Little People, BIG DREAMS™
HEDY LAMARR

Written by
Maria Isabel Sánchez Vegara

Illustrated by
Maggie Cole

Frances Lincoln
Children's Books

Long ago, there was a bright little girl in Vienna, Austria, called Hedwig. She loved to sit next to her father by the fire and listen to incredible stories about how machines and engines worked.

Her favorite hobby was working on her own
inventions ... like a dog collar that would glow
in the dark! In a notebook, Hedwig wrote down
stunning ideas that were ahead of her time.

At school, her teachers were amazed by this clever young girl. But those who didn't know her couldn't see beyond her face. Hedwig was just the most beautiful girl they had ever seen.

She was taking acting lessons in Vienna when
she got her first job as a member of a film crew.
It didn't take long for a film director to notice her
and offer Hedwig a role as an extra in his next movie.

Hedwig was 18 when she played the main role in an unusual film for the time. Her parents and the whole movie theater were shocked to see her swimming in a lake without any clothes. It was something never shown in a movie before.

She fell in love with a rich arms dealer called Friedrich, who turned out to be a jealous and controlling husband. He even forced her to quit acting! Hedwig, who was a free spirit, felt like a bird captured in a golden cage.

Every now and then, her husband invited his colleagues home. They would talk about terrible weapons and new military technologies in front of Hedwig, thinking that Friedrich's beautiful wife could not understand a word.

When Friedrich decided to celebrate a dinner for
his best clients, Hedwig knew it was the chance
she had been waiting for ... she had a plan!
First, she wore all of her jewelry.

Then, she disguised herself as a maid and escaped from her unbearable husband! Carrying just a single suitcase, Hedwig traveled to America. She was about to start a new life in Hollywood as the great actress Hedy Lamarr!

The day her first film was released,
Hedy became a box-office sensation.

Everybody left the movie theater thinking she was the most glamorous woman ever seen on a screen.

Yet Hedy kept creating new inventions from her Beverly Hills home. When the war started in Europe, she worked with a musician called George on a radio-signaling device. They called it the "Secret Communication System."

Hedy and George donated their device to the US military to help fight the Nazis.

Little could they imagine that their invention would become the basis of the wireless internet technology that we use today.

And by always trying to do much more than anyone
expected from her, little Hedy became not only one
of the greatest Hollywood actresses of her time,
but the most glamorous inventor
the world has ever met.

HEDY LAMARR

(Born 1914 – Died 2000)

1919

1938

Hedwig Eva Maria Kiesler was born in Vienna, Austria, on November 9, 1914. An only child, Hedwig occupied herself by reading and listening to her father's teachings about science. A brilliant student, she loved playing piano and ballet, and could speak four languages by the age of 10. Hedwig realized that acting was her real passion and, at 15, she was cast as an extra in the 1930 film *Money on the Street*. A year later, she moved to Berlin to study acting and her fame rose. Hedwig featured in a number of high-profile films, including a controversial movie in which she appeared naked. However, after marrying Friedrich "Fritz" Mandl in 1933, her career came to a sudden stop. Friedrich, an arms dealer who sold weapons to Nazi Germany, was a controlling and jealous husband, and forbade her

1940

c. 1960s

from acting. After four years of unhappiness, Hedwig fled her marriage and left for the US. There, she changed her name to Hedy Lamarr, inspired by a silent film star called Barbara La Marr, and became one of the biggest celebrities in Hollywood. Alongside her acting career, Hedy was an inventor and teamed up with her friend, George Antheil. Using a self-playing piano, they created a device that emitted a frequency-hopping signal designed to protect the airplanes of Allied forces during World War Two. The invention was never used for this purpose, but it informed the development of technology that is still used today. In 2014, the pair were inducted into the National Inventors Hall of Fame. And twenty years after her death, a satellite named in Hedy's honor was launched into space.

Want to find out more about **Hedy Lamarr?**

Have a read of this great book:

Hedy Lamarr's Double Life

by Laurie Wallmark

Brimming with creative inspiration, how-to projects, and useful information to enrich your everyday life, quarto.com is a favorite destination for those pursuing their interests and passions.

Text © 2022 Maria Isabel Sánchez Vegara. Illustrations © 2022 Maggie Cole.

Original concept of the series by Maria Isabel Sánchez Vegara, published by Alba Editorial, SLU.

Little People, BIG DREAMS" and "Pequeña & Grande" are trademarks of Alba Editorial S.L.U. and/or Beautifool Couple S.L.

First Published in the USA in 2023 by Frances Lincoln Children's Books, an imprint of The Quarto Group.

Quarto Boston North Shore, 100 Cummings Center, Suite 265D, Beverly, MA 01915, USA

Tel: +1 978-282-9590, Fax: +1 978-283-2742 www.Quarto.com

A catalogue record for this book is available from the Library of Congress

ISBN 978-0-7112-4669-0

Set in Futura BT.

Published by Katie Cotton and Peter Marley • Designed by Sasha Moxon
Edited by Lucy Menzies • Production by Nikki Ingram
Editorial Assistance from Rachel Robinson
Manufactured in Guangdong, China CC082022
1 3 5 7 9 8 6 4 2

Photographic acknowledgements (pages 28-29, from left to right): 1. Actress Hedy Lamarr at Six © John Springer Collection/CORBIS/Corbis via Getty Images 2. Hedy Lamarr, movie star, nominated by Toni Frissell, fashion photographer. © Bettmann via Getty Images 3. Hedy Lamarr (1913 - 2000) poses for a portrait during a publicity shoot in Hollywood around 1940. © Transcendental Graphics via Getty Images 4. Hedy Lamarr, circa 1960s © Everett Collection Inc via Alamy Stock Photo

Collect the Little People, BIG DREAMS™ series:

FRIDA KAHLO	**COCO CHANEL** 	**MAYA ANGELOU**	**AMELIA EARHART**	**AGATHA CHRISTIE**	**MARIE CURIE**	**ROSA PARKS**	**AUDREY HEPBURN**
EMMELINE PANKHURST	**ELLA FITZGERALD** 	**ADA LOVELACE** 	**JANE AUSTEN** 	**GEORGIA O'KEEFFE**	**HARRIET TUBMAN**	**ANNE FRANK**	**MOTHER TERESA** 
JOSEPHINE BAKER 	**L. M. MONTGOMERY**	**JANE GOODALL**	**SIMONE DE BEAUVOIR**	**MUHAMMAD ALI**	**STEPHEN HAWKING**	**MARIA MONTESSORI**	**VIVIENNE WESTWOOD**
MAHATMA GANDHI	**DAVID BOWIE**	**WILMA RUDOLPH**	**DOLLY PARTON**	**BRUCE LEE**	**RUDOLF NUREYEV**	**ZAHA HADID** 	**MARY SHELLEY**
MARTIN LUTHER KING JR.	**DAVID ATTENBOROUGH**	**ASTRID LINDGREN**	**EVONNE GOOLAGONG**	**BOB DYLAN** 	**ALAN TURING** 	**BILLIE JEAN KING** 	**GRETA THUNBERG**
JESSE OWENS	**JEAN-MICHEL BASQUIAT**	**ARETHA FRANKLIN**	**CORAZON AQUINO**	**PELÉ**	**ERNEST SHACKLETON** 	**STEVE JOBS**	**AYRTON SENNA**
LOUISE BOURGEOIS 	**ELTON JOHN** 	**JOHN LENNON**	**PRINCE**	**CHARLES DARWIN**	**CAPTAIN TOM MOORE**	**HANS CHRISTIAN ANDERSEN** 	**STEVIE WONDER**

MEGAN RAPINOE · MARY ANNING · MALALA YOUSAFZAI · ANDY WARHOL · RUPAUL · MICHELLE OBAMA · MINDY KALING · IRIS APFEL

ROSALIND FRANKLIN · RUTH BADER GINSBURG · MARILYN MONROE · KAMALA HARRIS · ALBERT EINSTEIN · CHARLES DICKENS · YOKO ONO · MICHAEL JORDAN

NELSON MANDELA · PABLO PICASSO · AMANDA GORMAN · GLORIA STEINEM · FLORENCE NIGHTINGALE · HARRY HOUDINI · J.R.R. TOLKIEN · ELVIS PRESLEY

NEIL ARMSTRONG · ALEXANDER VON HUMBOLDT · NIKOLA TESLA · WILMA MANKILLER · MARCUS RASHFORD · LAVERNE COX · MAE JEMISON · DWAYNE JOHNSON

HELEN KELLER · ANNA PAVLOVA · QUEEN ELIZABETH · TERRY FOX · HEDY LAMARR

ACTIVITY BOOKS

STICKER ACTIVITY BOOK · COLORING BOOK · LITTLE ME, BIG DREAMS JOURNAL

Discover more about the series at www.littlepeoplebigdreams.com